Stark County District Library
www.StarkLibrary.org
330.452.0665

NOV   2014

D1274582

XTREME FISH

Barracuda

BY S.L. HAMILTON

A&D Xtreme
An imprint of Abdo Publishing | www.abdopublishing.com

Visit us at
www.abdopublishing.com

Published by Abdo Publishing Company, a division of ABDO, PO Box 398166, Minneapolis, Minnesota 55439. Copyright ©2015 by Abdo Consulting Group, Inc. International copyrights reserved in all countries. No part of this book may be reproduced in any form without written permission from the publisher. A&D Xtreme™ is a trademark and logo of Abdo Publishing Company.

Printed in the United States of America, North Mankato, Minnesota.
042014
092014

PRINTED ON RECYCLED PAPER

Editor: John Hamilton
Graphic Design: Sue Hamilton
Cover Design: Sue Hamilton
Cover Photo: Getty Images
Interior Photos: AP-pgs 14-15; Corbis-pgs 8-9 & 26-27; Getty Images-pgs 4-5, 6-7 (bottom), 12, & 28-29; Glow Images-pgs 1, 13 (middle & bottom), 18-19 & 24-25; National Oceanic and Atmospheric Administration-pgs 22-23; RavenFire Media-pgs 6-7 (top); Science Source-pgs 10-11 (top) & 20-21; Silver Image Photo Agency-pg 27 (inset); Thinkstock-pgs 2-3, 10-11 (bottom), 13 (top), 16-17, 30-31 & 32.

Websites
To learn more about Xtreme Fish, visit booklinks.abdopublishing.com. These links are routinely monitored and updated to provide the most current information available.

Library of Congress Control Number: 2014932239

Cataloging-in-Publication Data

Hamilton, S. L.
  Barracuda / S. L. Hamilton.
   p. cm. -- (Xtreme fish)
Includes index.
ISBN 978-1-62403-446-6
1. Barracudas--Juvenile literature.   2. Marine animals--Juvenile literature.
3. Predatory animals--Juvenile literature. I. Title.
597/.7--dc23

2014932239

Contents

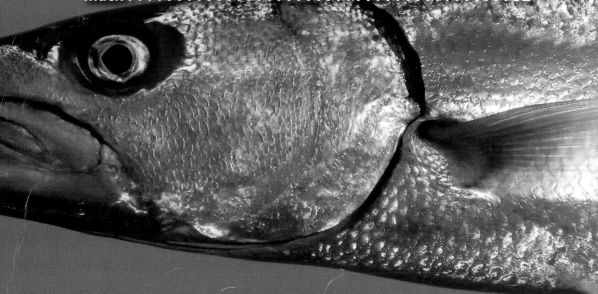

Barracuda

Barracuda are fast and agile. They are long and sleek, as streamlined as a submarine. They are also fierce predators. Their mouths are full of sharp teeth. These saltwater fish can snap their prey in half in a single bite.

XTREME FACT –
Barracuda are sometimes
called the "Tigers of the Sea."

Species & Location

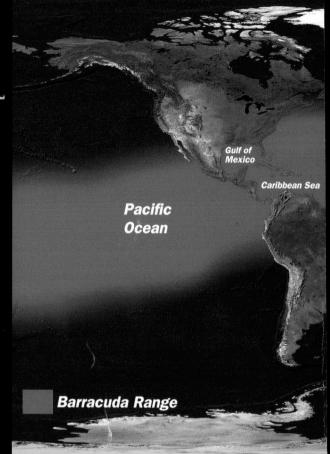

Pacific Ocean

Gulf of Mexico

Caribbean Sea

Barracuda Range

There are more than 20 species of barracuda. They have existed on Earth for about 20 million years. Barracuda are found in the warm waters of the Atlantic Ocean, Gulf of Mexico, Caribbean Sea, Mediterranean Sea, Red Sea, as well as parts of the Indian Ocean and Pacific Ocean.

A barracuda fossil.

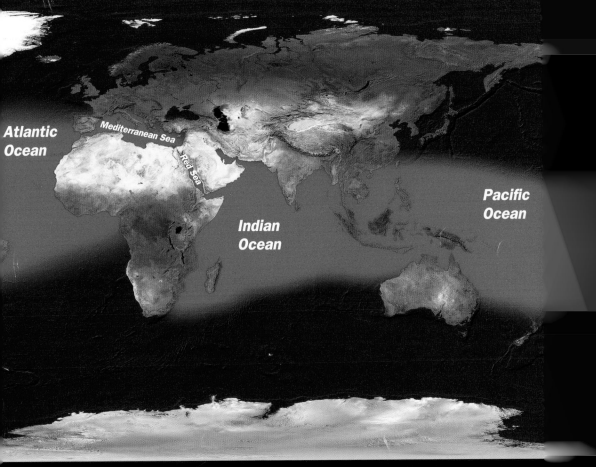

Atlantic Ocean

Mediterranean Sea

Red Sea

Indian Ocean

Pacific Ocean

Most barracuda prefer to live near tropical coastlines. In these locations there are sea grasses, mangroves, lagoons, and coral reefs. Prey fish are plentiful in these areas.

Size

Barracuda may grow to great sizes. They typically grow to 2 feet (.6 m) in length and weigh 88 pounds (40 kg). One of the largest barracuda caught by an angler was a record 5.5 feet (1.7 m). It weighed 103 pounds (47 kg). It is estimated that one species, great barracuda, may grow up to 6.6 feet (2 m) long. They live up to 14 years.

XTREME FACT– Barracuda usually live near the water's surface, but may swim as deep as 325 feet (99 m).

Shape

Barracuda are shaped to move at great speeds. Their pointed heads and aerodynamic bodies easily cut through the water, propelled by a powerful tail. They can also move vertically up and down through the water by inflating or deflating their swim bladder.

An x-ray of a barracuda.

XTREME FACT– Barracuda may swim as fast as 27 to 36 miles per hour (43 to 58 kph) in short bursts of speed.

Coloring

Depending on the species, adult barracuda range in color from tones of brown to blue-gray to silver-green. Newly hatched barracuda larvae look nothing like their future shape. Young barracuda can change their shades of color to match their surroundings. This unique camouflage helps protect them from predators.

A young barracuda in a mangrove swamp.

Juvenile barracuda hide among other fish.

Great barracuda can be identified by the black spots on their lower sides.

Pickhandle barracuda have dark stripes that make them look like pickaxe handles.

Yellowtail barracuda have a long yellow streak that ends in a yellow tail fin. This streak fades in older fish.

Eyesight

Barracuda are most active during the day. They use the light and their good eyesight to find their prey. A barracuda easily sees the silver or white flashes of a fish's scales or belly.

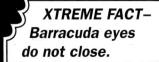

XTREME FACT–
Barracuda eyes
do not close.

Teeth & Jaws

A barracuda has a large mouth with two sets of gleaming teeth. The outside row are small, but razor-sharp. The inner row are the barracuda's large fang-like teeth. These huge teeth fit into holes in the opposite jaw. This lets the fish close its mouth and trap its prey.

A barracuda's fierce teeth are controlled by its powerful jaw muscles. When a barracuda strikes its prey at high speed, the fish is forced deep into the barracuda's open jaws. Once the prey hits the back of the mouth, the barracuda's jaw muscles are triggered, slamming the mouth shut. The sharp-toothed jaws scissor the prey in half.

Sense of Smell

Although a barracuda mostly depends on its excellent eyesight to hunt for prey, it does have a good sense of smell. Its olfactory system detects scents in the water and sends messages to the barracuda's brain to alert it to possible nearby meals.

XTREME FACT– *While predators such as sharks can smell a drop of blood in the water from a great distance, barracuda depend on their eyesight. Their eyesight is so sharp, they can even detect tiny flashes of reflected light from a fish's scales.*

Lateral Line

Barracuda have a body part called a lateral line. This organ allows them to sense objects around them. It runs from head to tail along its sides.

Lateral Line

The lateral line helps barracuda feel movement in the water. They can tell when prey are nearby.

Hunting

Barracuda often swim near the water's surface. With their excellent eyesight, they can get a good view of the surrounding area. A barracuda will pick out its prey and then wait. When the prey is no longer paying attention, the barracuda races down and chomps its victim. If the prey hasn't been killed, the barracuda will turn, bite down, and shake its lunch to kill it. This is known as "ram-biting."

XTREME FACT– Barracuda are good hunters, but they are also scavengers. They will follow larger fish, such as sharks, and take pieces of whatever the shark is eating.

What Barracuda Eat

Barracuda eat other fish such as jacks, grunts, groupers, snappers, small tuna, mullets, killifishes, herrings, and anchovies.

XTREME FACT – Except for humans, barracuda have few predators. Sharks, tuna, killer whales, and grouper eat adult barracuda. Small barracuda become prey for many other larger fish. But as they grow, they become the predators.

Barracuda also eat shrimp, crustaceans, octopus, and squid. They are not afraid to go after really large fish. Barracuda use a triple-strike approach to eating. First, a barracuda snaps a fish in half. The second and third approaches allow it to eat one half and then the other half of the prey.

A barracuda attacks a ball of herring.

Attacks on Humans

Humans are not a barracuda's first meal choice. Although it is rare, barracudas do attack swimmers and divers. Usually, it is thought that the barracuda are either protecting themselves, or it's a case of mistaken identity in murky waters.

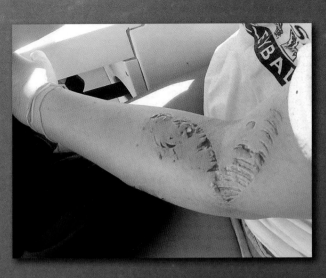

A teenage girl's arm shows the bite marks from a barracuda swimming off the coast of Florida.

XTREME FACT – Divers often see barracuda following them. Some scientists believe that barracuda think of the divers as big predators. Since barracuda are scavengers, they hope to get the leftovers from the bigger "fish" (divers). Other scientists believe that barracuda use divers as a distraction. They hide behind the divers, then dart out to get their prey.

Fishing for Barracuda

People catch barracuda as a sport fish and for food. These fish are sought with hook and line. Hooks are baited with everything from small live fish to flies.

In boats, anglers troll at speeds
of 5 knots (6 mph/9 kph).
Barracuda chase the lure.
Once hooked, barracuda
will fight fiercely.

Glossary

AERODYNAMIC
Something that has a shape that reduces the drag, or resistance, of air or water moving across its surface. Fish with aerodynamic shapes can go faster because they don't have to push as hard to move through the water.

AGGRESSIVE
Likely to attack, with or without a reason to do so.

CAMOUFLAGE
Coloring on clothing, skin, or fur that allows a creature to blend in with its surroundings.

LARVAE
The plural form of larva, the worm-like form of a newly hatched creature, such as an insect or a fish.

LATERAL LINE
A visible line that runs along the sides of fish. It helps fish detect movement in the water. The sensing organ helps fish to find prey and avoid becoming prey themselves.

OLFACTORY
Olfactory refers to the sense of smell.

SCAVENGERS

Creatures that eat what they can find, including dead and dying prey, or prey stolen from another animal's kill.

SPORT FISH

A type of fish that anglers hunt because of its fierceness and difficulty in landing, making its capture an exciting sport. Barracuda are a sport fish.

STREAMLINED

The shape of a creature or object that reduces the drag, or resistance, of air or water flowing across its surface. This increases speed and ease of movement. Fish, such as barracuda, have a streamlined shape that allows them to swim faster because they don't have to push as hard to move through the water.

SWIM BLADDER

A sac inside the body of a fish that holds air. It is also known as a gas bladder or air bladder. It helps a fish move vertically up and down in the water.

TROLL

To fish by trailing a baited hook and line behind a moving boat.

Index